Original title:
The Chlorophyll Chronicles

Copyright © 2025 Creative Arts Management OÜ
All rights reserved.

Author: Evelyn Hartman
ISBN HARDBACK: 978-1-80566-594-6
ISBN PAPERBACK: 978-1-80566-879-4

Serene Symphony of Chlorophyll

In a forest where leaves giggle,
Squirrels dance, oh so spry.
Moss plays the accordion lightly,
While dandelions underhandedly sigh.

Breeze blows through tree branches,
Whispering secrets to the sun.
Frogs croak out funny jokes,
As nature's stand-up has begun.

The raccoons wear tiny hats,
As they rummage through the bins.
With a wink and a nod they laugh,
While plotting their next wins.

And when the night takes over,
Fireflies start their glow.
Their winks are like tiny giggles,
In this forest comedy show.

Breaths of Nature's Spirit

The flowers hold a summit,
Debating who's the best smell.
Daisies giggle at the roses,
Who boast and brag so well.

The grass holds tickle contests,
As bugs buzz on mini swings.
Leaves create a leafy chorus,
As nature joyfully sings.

A hedgehog dons a cape,
Pretending he can fly.
While butterflies in tutus float,
Through the bright blue sky.

Nature's breath is full of laughs,
In this enchanting scene.
For those who pause and listen close,
Will find the funny green.

Whispers of Verdant Dreams

In the glade of leafy whispers,
Trees gossip with the breeze.
"Did you hear about the acorn?
He thinks he's a mighty freeze!"

Frogs wear crowns made of lilies,
To rule their mini pond.
They croak out royal decrees,
And let the dragonflies respond.

The sunbeams do a shimmy,
As clouds join in to play.
Nature's stage is set for fun,
In a bright and breezy way.

And when the moon comes shining,
All critters cease their schemes.
With laughter fading softly,
In the realm of verdant dreams.

In the Embrace of Green

Moss-laden rocks wear blankets,
As the stream hums a tune.
Butterflies join an orchestra,
Under the watchful moon.

The shade of trees is gentle,
Tickling toes of those who rest.
While ants march with a mission,
To prove they're nature's best.

Each plant tells a story,
Of sunlight, rain, and glee.
In this embrace of green delight,
Life dances merrily.

With laughter in the meadows,
And joy beneath the trees,
Nature speaks in giggles,
In a symphony of glee.

Nature's Silent Narratives

In the garden, plants conspire,
With whispers only they inspire.
A sunflower giggles up so high,
While roses roll their eyes and sigh.

The daisies dance in subtle glee,
Unseen jokes from leaf to tree.
A fern feigns a sneeze in jest,
While mushrooms chuckle in their nest.

Illuminations in the Understory

Beneath the canopy, shadows play,
Moss giggles, all in disarray.
A beetle wearing shades so cool,
Claims it's the king of the woodland school.

Glowing fungi hold a rave,
Roots dance like they're misbehave.
The gloom's alive with crazy pranks,
Where squirrels join in, giving thanks.

The Poetry of Photosynthesis

Leaves stretch out to catch some sun,
In this green world, laughter's fun!
Photosynthesis is quite the show,
Where plants tell jokes as light does flow.

Chloroplasts whisper lines in rhyme,
As they convert the light through time.
With carbon they play a witty game,
While oxygen cheers, "I'm to blame!"

Roots, Stems, and Stories

Roots dig deep, with tales to tell,
Of hidden treasures, where stories dwell.
Stems boast their height, with swagger and flair,
While leaves roll in laughter, floating in air.

"Who's the tallest?" the branches contest,
"Let's settle this in a windy jest!"
Buds pop open with giggles, you see,
Nature's own stand-up comedy!

The Leaf's Unwritten Script

Once a leaf, bold and bright,
always dreamed of taking flight.
It tried to jump, it wore a smile,
only to land in a puddle awhile.

With friends, it formed a leafy crew,
plotting adventures just for dew.
They schemed to ride a breeze so strong,
but ended up stuck in a bird's song.

Each gust was met with goofy glee,
as they danced on a bumblebee.
But dangling high from a twig so fine,
they laughed about sipping sap like wine.

Oh, the tales of the leafy clan,
finding joy in a simple plan.
A crumpled map and a cheerful cheer,
these leaves live well, year after year.

Wandering through the Woodland Stories

In the woods, where shadows play,
tiwnog squirrels plot their escapade.
They hide acorns in a line,
hoping to find a treasure divine.

A raccoon with a mask so sly,
caught on camera, oh my, oh my!
With a snack find that's quite absurd,
he giggles at a wandering bird.

An owl with glasses reads a tome,
"Best practices for a woodland home."
But every time it tries to share,
it falls asleep—oh, the woodland flair!

Through twisty trees, they all convene,
a critter council, quite the scene!
Their laughter echoes, wild and free,
for mischief thrives in their canopy.

Threads of Green and Gold

Threads of green spun with cheer,
bound to make the world appear.
The bumblebees wear party hats,
while butterflies have dance-offs with cats.

In the blend of leaf and sun,
the colors clash—such jolly fun!
A chipmunk winks, it's all a joke,
as it nudges a leafy folk.

Each sunrise paints a vibrant scene,
always shifting, fresh and keen.
Laughter sprouts from every plan,
as nature spins its playful yarn.

With tendrils twirling, hearts so bold,
these threads weave tales in green and gold.
A tapestry of rumbling glee,
singing songs of leaves and trees.

Harmonies of the Forest Floor

On the forest floor, where critters roam,
a tongue-in-cheek woodsy home.
The mushrooms hum a happy tune,
while ants tap dance beneath the moon.

Frogs croak classics, frogs with flair,
they ripple tunes in moist cool air.
A hedgehog croons in hushed delight,
turning sticks into a mic for the night.

Dancing shadows, the trees engage,
each branch a part of the lively stage.
With swaying laughter, they pull you in,
as acorns bounce—let the show begin!

So come, dear friend, to the forest floor,
where harmonies dwell, forever more.
With every step, a giggle found,
a ballet of nature spins all around.

Whispers of the Leafy Lore

In the garden, plants conspire,
Telling secrets, never tire.
A cabbage winks, a carrot grins,
While spinach waits, and giggles spins.

A dandelion declares a race,
With tulips trying to keep pace.
They laugh and rustle, sway with glee,
In their own green jubilee!

Tapestry of Nature's Hues

Oh, look at the colors intertwined,
Each petal's story, nicely aligned.
A daisy with a polka dot dress,
Says, 'I'm the fairest, I must confess!'

While wintergreen rolls with a cheer,
And the violets grin ear to ear.
They barter gossip, trade some cheer,
In this bright patch of green frontier!

Shades of Growth and Reflection

A fern bends low, whispers, 'Hey!'
A wise old oak joins in the play.
They joke about the breeze's fun,
And argue if it's two against one.

The sunlight winks, a radiant tease,
While beetles buzz in giggly ease.
In moments fleeting, funny yet grand,
The leaves all join, hand in hand.

Echoes in the Emerald Shade

Beneath the shade, the lizards laugh,
As daisies map out their own path.
Insects dance, a quirky ballet,
Swaying with joy, come what may.

A sly chipmunk, with nuts in tow,
Cracks jokes only the plants know.
They share a chuckle, warm and light,
In their green world, everything's bright!

Beneath the Verdure

In gardens thick with glee and green,
The flowers dance, a vibrant scene.
The lazy bees buzz by with flair,
While ants march on, without a care.

A snail slips through, all slick and slow,
With dreams of cheese to steal the show.
The daisies giggle in the breeze,
As roots conspire beneath the trees.

The squirrels plot their nutty schemes,
While creaky branches share their dreams.
A romping puppy joins the race,
Chasing shadows in this leafy space.

With nature's laughter all around,
In verdant hues, such joy is found.
So take a breath, let worries cease,
And join the fun, embrace the peace.

The Leaf's Silent Saga

A leaf once told a tale profound,
Of whispers shared from ground to ground.
It fancied itself a mighty ship,
Sailing through air on a breezy trip.

The wind was its mischievous mate,
Promising fun, oh it couldn't wait!
But then a storm, fierce and bold,
Left it spinning, feeling cold.

The leaf lamented its lofty dreams,
While clouds above plotted in teams.
Yet once the sun broke through the gray,
It danced once more, come what may.

So if you see a leaf take flight,
Know it's chasing joy, pure delight.
With every flutter, every sway,
It's telling secrets in a playful way.

Awakening the Green Spirit

In early morn, the sun peeks through,
Awakening greens in bright, fresh dew.
The frogs begin their concert loud,
While worms wiggle, oh so proud.

A raccoon dons a leafy hat,
While birds gossip, just imagine that!
The flowers stretch with yawns so wide,
As butterflies dart on a joyride.

The grass blades giggle, tickling toes,
While shadows play in leafy clothes.
Laughter bubbles from the brook,
As nature gasps and takes a look.

In this realm where humor thrives,
The spirit of green joyfully drives.
So come and join this merry spree,
Under the sun, so wild and free!

A Tapestry Woven in Leaves

A tapestry of green unfurls,
With threads of laughter, spins and twirls.
The branches whisper cheeky rhymes,
As nature giggles through the times.

The ferns are dressed in fancy fronds,
While mushrooms laugh at silly ponds.
A rabbit hops in clumsy joy,
Stealing snacks from a picnic's ploy.

The sunbeams peek through leafy lace,
Creating shadows—a playful chase.
The squirrels argue over acorn SEO,
"Mine's the best; no, really, don't you know?"

So stitch together this leafy cheer,
Where every creature's heart is clear.
In this patchwork of green and fun,
Life dances beneath the glowing sun.

Leafy Legends Unfold

In the forest, leaves conspire,
Whispering gossip through the briar.
'Did you see that squirrel's new dance?'
'This party tree needs a nice prance!'

Branches shake, laughter takes flight,
Sunbeams giggle, a joyous sight.
Rabbits hop in stylish shoes,
As daisies debate the latest news.

A clever vine with a sly grin,
Keeps tally of who's the best kin.
'You call that growth? That's just a sprout!'
'Oh please, isn't this what it's about?'

As twilight falls and shadows blend,
They toast with acorns, no need to pretend.
In every rustle, a jest does bloom,
The forest's folly, a leafy room.

Chronicles of the Photosynthetic Heart

In a meadow, green folks convene,
Each blade with a tale, quite obscene.
'Yo, why does grass always stay low?'
'It's too afraid of a garden hoe!'

Bees buzz near, with sweet little prattles,
'Who's the best pollinator? Let's settle!'
Butterflies flutter with colorful flair,
'In this show, I'm the diva rare!'

Ferns unfold their fronds with pride,
'My curls are better, you just can't hide!'
Moss sits back, all quiet and chill,
'It's not a competition, it's just a thrill!'

As day fades out, the crew takes a bow,
Under stars that twinkle, 'Wow!' they vow.
In this field of jest, where whispers start,
Lies a treasure, the photosynthetic heart.

Sylvan Stories in Bloom

Once in a glade, where sunshine spills,
A gnarled tree shares quirky thrills.
'Why did the leaf refuse to stay?'
'It couldn't leaf well, no way!'

Dewdrops giggle on petals bright,
As critters jam under the moonlight.
'Hey, let's start a band with rocks!'
'As long as you don't bring the socks!'

Vines dance wildly, twirling round,
While ferns shout verses, quite profound.
Each story told, a chuckle ensues,
In this leafy world, joy's the muse.

So join the fun, the tales untold,
In fragrant air that never gets old.
Where every leaf has a voice in dream,
Laughter echoes in nature's theme.

Nature's Painted Pages

On a canvas of green, colors collide,
With brushes of wind and water beside.
'Watch out for that spotted caterpillar!'
'He's just a painter, but much taller!'

Rippling rivers with fish in a race,
'Catch me if you can, let's quicken the pace!'
Lilies laugh with their sun-kissed attire,
While dragonflies buzz, igniting the fire.

A cheeky crow puts on a show,
Wings flapping raucously, stealing the glow.
'Mind your snacks, I'm on the prowl!'
And beneath the trees, a raucous howl.

As dusk paints the sky a vibrant hue,
Creatures gather for a grand debut.
From the roots deep, to branches so wide,
Nature's laughter, her joyful pride.

Emerald Whispers

In the garden, leaves do chatter,
Telling tales of bugs that splatter.
A worm wears glasses, oh so fine,
Claiming he's the smartest vine.

Frogs dance wildly to the beat,
While ants march on with tiny feet.
Each flower giggles, oh what fun,
As breezes join in, a wild run.

Rabbits pause with curious eyes,
Wondering why the grass is wise.
"Let's party," shouts a sunflower bright,
As daylight fades into the night.

So, if you hear these whispers green,
Join the plants in their silly scene.
For laughter blooms in every patch,
And nature's jokes are quite the catch!

Tales of the Verdant Veil

In the woods where shadows play,
Trees gossip in a leafy way.
A squirrel tells a riddle true,
"Why don't mushrooms ever stew?"

The vines twist round in playful glee,
As bees explain their honey spree.
"Life's a picnic," says a ladybug,
"Until you find a thorny hug!"

Sunlight tickles every leaf's face,
Calling forth a dance, a race.
"Chop chop!" says the busy ant,
"Time for lunch, don't be so scant!"

So heed the tales the foliage spins,
Celebrate the laughter that begins.
In nature's mirth, we find our way,
Amidst the green, we laugh and play.

Lush Secrets Beneath

What's beneath, oh roots of cheer?
A party starts when night is near.
Mice in hats throw a surprise,
While fireflies light up the skies.

A hedgehog croons a silly song,
While worms harmonize all night long.
"Let's drink from dew," the beetles cheer,
And toast to gardens filled with cheer!

Underneath, where shadows creep,
Nature's secrets start to leap.
"Here's to grass with tangy zest!"
A cluster cheers, "We're truly blessed!"

So when you wander, stop and see,
The fun beneath, so wild and free.
For laughter echoes underground too,
In this green realm made for you.

Green Guardians of the Glade

Once upon a leafy time,
Guardians danced in jazz, a rhyme.
Bark-clad gnomes with twinkling eyes,
Spotted fairies in disguise.

"Quick!" said one, "Let's spin around!"
As mushrooms sprouted from the ground.
Each leaf swirled with giggles loud,
Nature's mischief, oh so proud!

A wise old oak told tales of yore,
Of wacky quests and plant folklore.
"Did you hear?" a willow sighed,
"Last week, the flower pot just cried!"

So if you roam where green things grow,
Remember the stories they bestow.
For laughter reigns in every glade,
With green guardians unafraid!

Greenstone Chronicles

In the forest, leaves conspire,
With whispers loud, they conspire.
The squirrels plot, the birds all laugh,
As trees and grass draw a quick graph.

A clumsy frog jumps, slips on dew,
He croaks, "Hey, that's not a shoe!"
While gnomes in gardens sip their tea,
They nod and say, "Oh, let it be!"

Underneath the sprawling shade,
A snail reveres his slow parade.
He dreams of races while he creeps,
And laughs as faster friends take leaps.

In laughter's shade, the flowers quirk,
They sway and dance, just going berserk.
A butterfly steals the show, you see,
As all the blooms shout, "Look at me!"

Dance of the Sunlit Canopy

Up in the trees, where the sunlight spills,
The leaves do jiggles, the breeze gives thrills.
Branches swing to a rhythm divine,
While birds string notes like a fine wine.

A chipmunk twirls with acorn in hand,
Declaring, "This is the best in the land!"
He spins and hops, a fuzzy ballet,
While squirrels clap, shouting, "Hooray!"

A ray of sun sneaks down to boast,
"I'm golden glory, I'm the most!"
But shadows laugh, in their cool gown,
Saying, "Don't fret, you wear a frown!"

Dappled light marks this canopy's game,
Where laughter's the rule and fun is the aim.
They giggle, they shimmy, but all know the truth,
Nature's the kid that won in their youth.

Memories Among the Moss

Among the moss, tales softly glow,
Of mushrooms chatting, and dandelions' show.
A rabbit hums a forgotten tune,
While shadows jest under the moon.

From tiny toadstools, a council meets,
Debating who'll steal the next spring's sweets.
"Not me!" croaks a frog, with a wink and a jig,
"Last time it led to a dance so big!"

Mossy memories, the tales they weave,
Where even the snails take time to grieve.
They reminisce of a squirrel's lost hat,
"Who wears a hat?" probes a curious cat.

So here's to the stories, all fuzzy and green,
Where laughter echoes, always serene.
In the heart of the woods, let's cheer and toast,
To friendly weeds and the moss that we boast!

The Essence of Green Dreams

In every sprout, a giggle grows,
In every bud, the laughter flows.
The carrots joke, "We're underground stars!"
As they wiggle their leaves and whisper "Hooray, ours!"

Beneath the green, a worm gives a cheer,
Saying, "Underground, you've nothing to fear!"
The roots all chuckle, they twist and they turn,
While moles make mischief, and young shoots yearn.

A dandy lily, all poised and neat,
Says, "I'm the finest, come take a seat!"
But daisies giggle, "We're wild and free!"
As they sway in the breeze, just as they please.

In dreamlike woods where whimsy reigns,
Nature's humor glitters in daylight's chains.
Join the dance of green, let laughter proclaim,
That life's true magic is often a game!

Verdant Echoes of Yesterday

In a world where plants conspire,
Talking leaves gather and admire.
They gossip of soil and sunny days,
And chuckle at worms in silly ways.

The daisies dance, throwing a fit,
While broccoli sings, 'I'm quite a hit!'
Ferns roll their eyes at the dandelion,
Saying, 'What a puff! Is that a crime?'

A cactus pranks the passing bee,
'You're sweet but stuck, can't you see?'
While oak trees laugh with a creaky sound,
Sharing tales from the roots underground.

Oh, what a riot beneath our feet,
Where grass is alive with jokes to repeat!
Laughter frolics among the green,
As nature plays the silliest scene.

Grove of Forgotten Dreams

In a grove where the shadows play,
The acorns scheme, oh what a day!
They whisper dreams of mighty oaks,
While snickering at squirrel-y jokes.

The willow waves like a silly judge,
'Your growth is stunted, won't you budge?'
With fronds that tickle and roots that joke,
They laugh at the antics of an old oak.

A maple mocks with a bright red grin,
'Gonna lose your leaves? Let the fun begin!'
While apples tumble, giggling south,
Giving the worms a free lunch mouth.

At dusk, they hold a leafy ball,
With twinkling fireflies, one and all.
A party for plants, oh what a sight!
In the grove, all worries take flight.

The Song of Chloralight

In a meadow where green dreams hum,
A chorus of grasses—now that's some fun!
With crickets providing the bass in the night,
Every leaf sways as they reach for the light.

'Hey, clover, can you keep the beat?'
'Only if dandelion brings the heat!'
With melodies woven from sunbeams bright,
They sing till the moon steals the show tonight.

The peduncle strings rock out with flair,
While starlings join in, singing without care.
Bright blossoms shimmy, they wiggle and sway,
As nature's DJ spins leaves into play.

But watch out for weeds in their shifty shoes,
Trying to dance into the groove with the blues!
The song rolls on with a chuckle and cheer,
For in this garden, fun is always near.

Secrets of the Leafy Realm

In the leafy realm, where secrets abound,
A crabapple tree whispers all around.
'Did you hear the tulips swap names again?
Call me Joe—no wait, I'm Glen!'

The ferns exchange nods, full of delight,
'Gossiping roots, oh what a night!'
The honeysuckle climbs to join the chat,
Spilling the tea—'Who's that with the hat?'

Pumpkins boast of their orange hue,
While wildflowers share tales that are true.
'We sprouted from dreams, or so they claim,
Yet still can't recall from whence we came!'

As twilight settles, they toast with glee,
'To our leafy kingdom! We're wild and free!'
In the tangled laughter of nature's embrace,
The secrets of green bring a smile to each face.

Ode to the Green and Growing

In a garden thrives the weed,
A rebel plant with silly speed.
It dances in the morning sun,
And claims the title: "Weed is Fun!"

With leaves like fans, it cools the air,
Spreading joy without a care.
Petunia pouts, but dandelions grin,
"In this wild race, let's begin!"

Each stem a story, each leaf a laugh,
In tangled beds, they form their path.
The roses sigh, with pained delight,
While violets giggle, lost in the light.

So here's a toast to green delights,
To photosynthesis, wild flights.
May plants rejoice with every sprout,
And chuckle at what life's about!

Rhythms of Roots

Roots tapping into the earthen beat,
A funky dance beneath our feet.
Worms in time with the soil's bass,
Living down in this hidden space.

They wiggle and coil, oh what a sight,
In their underworld party, they dance all night.
With carrots as trumpets, and beets that can sing,
These earthy stars are the real spring fling!

So take a step, and feel the sound,
The heartbeat of life all around.
Each little root, a funky groove,
In the garden's nightclub, they absolutely move!

And as they sway, the earth claps back,
With every rhythm, the green grows thick.
In a world where even roots can jig,
Let's join the dance, come on, do a gig!

The Lushness of Existence

Each leaf a laugh, each bud a cheer,
Nature's humor rings so clear.
A cactus teased for being prickly,
Winks and jabs, oh, how utterly sickly!

Moss carpets the floor like nature's rug,
Inviting all, but oh so snug.
"Get comfy now, and take a seat!"
Says the toadstool, nonchalantly neat.

In lush green jungles where frogs sing tunes,
The flowers gossip about the moons.
"Who new bloomed last? What's the big buzz?"
Nature's chatter goes on because!

So here's to greenery that laughs and grows,
A funky fiesta, heaven knows!
Let's dance with mushrooms and giggle with trees,
For the lushness of life is a light-hearted tease!

Fables of Flora

Once a sunflower stood all tall,
Dreaming it could be a beach ball.
With petals fluffed and hopes so grand,
It bounced along, much to the land's reprimand.

The daisies whispered, "What a sight!"
"Thinking it's a game, how light!"
But oh how their laughter did mean,
The sunflower spun, living like a queen.

Tulips taught it how to sway,
To dance in winds that whisked all day.
With every wobble, the fun would rise,
In a garden world beneath bright skies.

For in this tale of flowers bold,
Joy is spread, and laughter unfolds.
So plant your dreams in the soil of cheer,
And join the fables, for summer is near!

Verdant Dreams and Nightmares

In the garden, plants conspire,
Telling tales of leafy fire.
A beetle dressed in dapper flair,
Waltzes round without a care.

Grasshoppers hold wild jam sessions,
While ants discuss their own obsessions.
But a snail slips in with quite a frown,
Claiming it's raining, so he sits down.

The daisies giggle, the roses pout,
As the worms throw a raucous shout.
Amidst the fun, the weeds run free,
An unruly bunch, oh woe is me!

In this dreamscape, where green rules rise,
Nature's humor is a grand surprise.
With laughter echoing through the air,
Verdant dreams dance without a care.

The Heartbeat of the Forest

High above, the owls take bets,
On who'll win the squirrel greensets.
While foxes gather, sharing jokes,
Telling tales of silly folks.

Beavers build with style and flair,
Constructing dams beyond compare.
The raccoons roam with bandit glee,
Planning pranks, oh can't you see?

Underneath the watery green,
Frogs hold court in a raucous scene.
Toads croak to the rhythm of the breeze,
Creating tunes that bring down trees.

So in this forest filled with cheer,
Nature laughs, it's loud and clear.
A heartbeat pulses in the night,
Reminding us that green feels right.

Leafy Legends of Old

Legends sprout from roots below,
Of trees that danced in stealthy glow.
The oak wore boots, the pine a cape,
With leafy tales hard to escape.

The whispers of the willow sway,
As crickets chirp their night ballet.
A wise old mushroom, in the dim,
Shares secrets, leaves us on a whim.

Bamboo bends with quite the tune,
While ferns toss hats to the moon.
Oh how the flowers chime in jest,
Claiming they are nature's best!

These legends spin through verdant days,
With laughter in a tangled maze.
In nature's heart, a tale unfolds,
Leafy laughter in whispers told.

The Art of Becoming Green

It starts with a flicker, a slide, a glide,
Learning from the lichen, we take it in stride.
The plants laugh together, teaching us well,
How to embrace the green that we sell.

Photosynthesizing on a wild dance floor,
The sun's rays are in, and the dark's out the door.
Caterpillars dream of their fashion shows,
In suits made of silk, oh how the green grows!

With each blossom, a chance to create,
An artistic palette shaped by fate.
Piecing together the hues of the earth,
Celebrating the joy of all things of worth.

So, join in the fun of this verdant scene,
Where everyone's crafty, and laughter's the theme.
In every leaf, the green spirit sings,
Mastering the art of what nature brings.

The Enigmas of Emerald Shadows

In the garden, shadows dance,
With plants that wear a leafy pants.
A squirrel debates, should he climb,
While grasshoppers laugh, keeping time.

The bushes gossip, can you hear?
Their whispers tickle, bring good cheer.
A rabbit hops, with flair so grand,
Declares he's king of this green land.

Cacti roll their eyes in place,
While daisies giggle, full of grace.
The twirling vines, they twist and twine,
As ivy waits to sip some wine.

So if you wander near the glade,
Embrace the quirks that plants have made.
For in the emerald shadows bright,
Life's funny tales bring pure delight.

A Serenade to the Green Spaces

In the park, the trees all sway,
Telling jokes in their leafy way.
The sunbeams play, a hide and seek,
While daisies nod with petals meek.

A turtle trots at half his speed,
Chasing a worm, that's quite the lead.
The bees hum tunes in busy flights,
While flowers nod in sheer delight.

The blossoms flaunt their colors bold,
Their vibrant stories waiting to be told.
A picnic spreads, with treats galore,
As ants march in like tiny chore.

So lift your gaze and laugh with glee,
Join in the fun, it's wild and free.
For nature's music, sweet and clear,
Will make you grin from ear to ear.

Days in the Orchard

In the orchard, apples grin,
Pears gossip about their kin.
The plums play peek-a-boo all day,
While cherries blush in bright array.

A hedgehog rolls, oh what a sight,
As peaches chuckle, feeling bright.
The lemons crack jokes, oh so sour,
While bees buzz in, like clockwork power.

The farmer hums a silly tune,
As leaves dance softly to the moon.
With every fruit, a tale to share,
In the orchard's fun, there's always care.

So savor life, take joy, and play,
In nature's rhythm, find your way.
For each sweet bite, a laugh you'll find,
In sunny orchards, hearts are kind.

The Unfolding of Green Stories

Among the ferns, tales swirl and twine,
Each leaf a page, a story line.
The rabbits sneer, in quiet mirth,
As daisies plot their secret birth.

With every breeze, the stories flip,
The ladybugs on ventures trip.
A watermelon weaves a plot,
While sunflowers boast of what they've got.

Each bud unfolds with giggles sweet,
As roots debate who's top of the feat.
The mushrooms chuckle, wise and old,
Holding secrets, stories bold.

So stroll along these green-filled trails,
Where laughter thrives, and joy prevails.
For every plant has tales to show,
Of fun in growth and nature's glow.

The Chronicles of Nature's Rebirth

In springtime's glow, the flowers giggle,
As tiny buds dance and wiggle.
The trees don green, a stylish spree,
While bees hum tunes in harmony.

The soil chuckles, rich and deep,
As worms do cartwheels, not a peep.
The sun winks down, a warm embrace,
Nature's stage, a funny place.

The streams run wild, they splash and dive,
With fish that leap to stay alive.
Each critter joins the comic show,
In nature's jest, we all can grow.

So raise a toast to leafy cheer,
To laughter shared with all we hold dear.
In every bloom, a smile is found,
In the vibrant world, joy does abound.

The Colors of Life Reclaimed

The sun spills paint on canvas skies,
While flowers bloom in quirky ties.
Dandelions sport their golden crowns,
As laughter echoes through the towns.

The butterflies strut in feathered flight,
With polka-dot wings, a charming sight.
They're nature's clowns in vivid hues,
Spreading joy like morning dews.

A rainbow sneezes, out pops green,
Which giggles as it's seldom seen.
The tadpoles wiggle, a slippery dance,
Turning ponds into a froggy trance.

Life's palette swirls in funny strokes,
With nature's voice, the world evokes.
From every leaf, a laugh takes wing,
In every drop, a song to sing.

Green Whispers in the Wind

The wind tells tales in rustling leaves,
Of squirrels plotting grand sheaves.
They sneak around with acorns bold,
In a treasure hunt that never gets old.

The grass grows tall, a ticklish feat,
As ants march home in a busy fleet.
They giggle softly, a tiny choir,
When raindrops fall like nature's fire.

The trees gossip, swaying with glee,
About the latest found bumblebee.
With branches linked in playful play,
They celebrate another sunny day.

So listen close to what they share,
In every breeze, a humorous flair.
Life's whispers dance, a joyful sound,
In nature's laughter, peace is found.

The Heart of the Woodlands

In the woodlands deep, where mischief brews,
Fairies giggle in sparkly shoes.
The raccoons roast marshmallows at night,
While owls hoot jokes in dim moonlight.

The branches sway, an awkward jig,
As chipmunks showcase every gig.
While rabbits hop with a comic twist,
In every leap, a chance not missed.

The mushrooms wear their polka-dot hats,
Inviting all the little brats.
They set up games of hide-and-seek,
Where whispers giggle and laughter sneak.

So wander here where fun takes flight,
The heart of woodlands, pure delight.
In every nook, a story's spun,
And nature's jest has just begun.

A Leaf's Lament

Oh, the sun said I'm a star,
But I'm just stuck in a jar.
With my pals, I do chime,
But they won't stop with the grime.

Green and bright, we sway and sway,
Waiting for the rain to play.
But when it pours, I start to fear,
Mud on my veins is rather sheer.

One breeze whispers, "Time to drop!"
But I can't dance, I'm stuck on top.
Life as a leaf is quite absurd,
Not all that glitter is green, I heard.

So here I hang, just clinging tight,
Wishing for a day that feels just right.
Laughing at ants who march below,
Oh, what a life, this leafy show!

The Rich Tapestry of Life

From acorns small to giants grand,
Nature makes a quirky band.
Mushrooms dance in purple shoes,
Even cacti sport their blues.

Raindrops fall like tiny bells,
Whispering secrets to the swells.
Each twig and berry plays a part,
Nature's comedy, pure art!

Squirrels hide their treasure chest,
While flowers bloom, and bees invest.
What's that noise? A chatter or hum?
Oh wait, just squirrels having fun!

Life unfolds in wacky ways,
Join the show, don't be a phase.
Trees in costumes, leaves in cheer,
Every season, a new premiere!

Chronicles of Wilderness Wisdom

Deep in the woods, wise branches sway,
They've seen more than most, they say.
Raccoons with masks, a sneaky lot,
Cackle at every dolphin thought.

The owls hoot in riddles galore,
"Why did the deer cross the forest floor?"
To laugh at the trees, they all can see,
Making friends by the old maple tree.

The river sings to the stones with glee,
While the sun plays tag with a bumblebee.
Every critter brings a giggle or joke,
Who knew a leaf could even poke?

So come listen to nature's sass,
The wild is fun—take a pass!
Old roots grumble, but trees delight,
In wilderness tales that ignite the night!

The Spirit of Growth

I sprouted up, what a sight!
But why do humans think I'm ripe?
They stop and stare, in awe they beam,
Little do they know, I'm living the dream.

In soil so rich, I wiggle and twist,
Each day in the sun, I can't resist.
Leaves pop out like fireworks bright,
Just wishing I could catch a flight.

But wait, there's a pest, a little bug!
Munching my leaves like it's a hug.
I rustle and shake, give a leafy cheer,
To show that I'm growing, never fear.

So I'll dance with the breeze, and sway with flair,
Each day a new chance to show I care.
In this world of green, I'll always glow,
Embracing the spirit, we all shall grow!

An Evergreen Epic

In a forest so lush, oh what a sight,
Every critter's dancing, full of delight.
Squirrels wear hats made of leaves just for fun,
While the wise old owl cracks jokes in the sun.

Trees tell tall tales as they sway in the breeze,
About how they once scared a herd of bees.
An acorn once tried to jump into fame,
But ended up stuck in a squirrel's game.

A raccoon with style, dressed in green couture,
Claims he's the best, but we know he's a bore.
Branches are giggling, their laughter won't cease,
Nature's own circus, oh what a masterpiece!

So come take a stroll, join in the glee,
Where the woods are alive with silly esprit.
Every leaf has a story, let's share in the cheer,
In this jolly green world, let's raise a cold beer!

Fables of the Ferns

Ferns whisper secrets in the hush of the night,
They know all the gossip, oh what a fright!
A snail once challenged a rabbit to race,
But it ended with mud on that poor bunny's face.

Mushrooms hold meetings on logs that they find,
Discussing the ways to be more open-minded.
One proposed pizza, the other, a stew,
Together they cooked up a plan meant for two.

In shadows, the chitchat, a riotous scene,
Toadstools are dreaming of being quite lean.
They diet on sunlight, or so they maintain,
While leaves are just laughing, "That's all in vain!"

So venture on and feast your own eyes,
On frolicking fables hidden 'neath skies.
In the land of the green, life's never routine,
Join the dance with the ferns and feel ever keen!

The Lore of Living Green

In a garden so bright, where colors collide,
Flowers wear sunglasses, it's quite a wild ride.
Bees buzz with rhythm, they're learning to groove,
And butterflies clap to the rhythm they move.

A tulip named Tim had a crush on the rose,
But his petals kept blushing, oh what a pose!
They shared funny stories about summer's hot glow,
While crafting a dance that amazed all below.

Wild vines climbed ladders, seeking higher ground,
In a race for the sun, who'd wear the crown?
But tangled in laughter, they fell in a heap,
A chorus of giggles, not one could keep sleep!

So wander and marvel at lush, vibrant scenes,
In this whimsical world, where joy's evergreen.
Each plant has a quirk, each bloom a big dream,
In the lore of the green, there's always a theme!

Journeys Through Canopied Realms

In the canopy high, where the monkeys convene,
Swinging through branches, they're quite the routine.
One claims he's the best at a somersault spin,
While his buddy just munches on leaves with a grin.

Parrots recite poetry, loud and absurd,
Squawking out rhymes that are truly unheard.
While groundhogs debate on the best type of snack,
And ponder the wisdom of living in shade's pack.

With critters adorning their costumes quite bright,
The dancing of shadows brings pure delight.
A hedgehog in spectacles recites olden tales,
About daring adventures in fairy-tale trails.

So sail through the leaves, in joy you'll be caught,
In this realm of green laughter, you'll find what you sought.
Every creature, a friend, every vine, a new song,
In the journeys through green, you truly belong!

Murmurs in the Meadow

In a meadow where flowers giggle,
Grasshoppers hold their wiggly wiggle.
A bumblebee hums a silly tune,
While daisies chat with the lazy moon.

The daisies declare it's time for tea,
But the wind insists, "Come dance with me!"
A squirrel joins in, with a little jig,
And the whole meadow laughs, oh so big!

Each blade of grass shares a cheeky grin,
While butterflies swirl in a jovial spin.
The clouds puff up, in a fluffy parade,
As the sun beams down, in sunshine cascade.

So join the frolic, your worries cease,
In this meadow of mirth, find your peace.
Nature's laughter is all around,
In a world where joy and fun abound!

Stories of the Twisting Vines

In the garden, the vines do twist,
Plotting mischief, oh, they can't resist.
Climbing high, they tickle the trees,
While shouting jokes carried by the breeze.

A tomato blushed, oh what a sight!
When a cucumber whispered, "You're quite ripe!"
The carrots chuckled, all snug in the ground,
Sharing puns that spun round and round.

Grapes rolled down, like a playful race,
"Catch us if you can!" they said with grace.
The pumpkins splashed in autumn's light,
Swinging their stems in a playful fight.

So gather 'round, hear the vine's tale,
Of laughter, fun, and not a dull detail.
In the garden's embrace, let spirits shine,
Join the frolic of stories divine!

An Ode to the Green Guardians

Oh, guardians clad in leafy attire,
With roots that dig deep, never tire.
They stand tall, wagging, arms out wide,
As squirrels parade, oh what a ride!

With whispers of leaves and a rustling cheer,
They gossip of critters that wander near.
Chirping birds throw in their two cents,
While awkward branches make no pretense.

"Who ordered a rain shower today?"
A wise old tree says, "I'd say hooray!"
But a playful gust shakes them about,
As they giggle and wiggle, there's no doubt.

So here's to the keepers of greenery bright,
With giggles and grins, they bring pure delight.
In the forest's embrace, so snug and round,
Lies the laughter of nature, so profound!

The Secret Life of Verdant Beings

In the hush of night, when the moon shines bright,
The green beings gather, oh what a sight!
Whispering secrets, they sway with glee,
In a dance so wild, it's hard to see.

The ferns plot mischief with toadstool friends,
"Let's leap on the squirrels and make amends!"
While the moss giggles as it spreads like a carpet,
In the moonlight glow, they hold a grand market.

Crickets play tunes with a tap-tap beat,
As the mushrooms waltz on their little feet.
"Did you hear the one about the old oak?"
They all burst out laughing, oh what a joke!

So next time you wander where shadows teem,
Listen closely and you might just dream.
Of verdant beings with hearts so light,
Living in laughter through the magical night!

Dancing Light in the Canopy

Sunbeams prance like little sprites,
Through leaves they twirl in playful flights.
A squirrel rolls by, with acorn in tow,
Shaking his tail, putting on quite the show.

A dance-off starts, with branches as stage,
Vines sway and twist, releasing their rage.
Frogs croak a rhythm, each one is a champ,
Bouncing and leaping, it's quite the damp stamp!

The shadows join in, a waltz of their own,
Making shapes that can't help but be shown.
A jam session starts with a woozy old bee,
Buzzing to tunes, oh what glee!

As the dusk settles, still giggles remain,
In the forest's heart, there's no time for pain.
So let's raise a toast to the leafy delight,
Under umbrellas of green, everything's bright!

Reverie of the Green Enclave

In a nook where green dreams sprout,
Bugs host a ball, there's no doubt.
Flies in tuxes, ladybugs shine,
Waltzing on leaves, feeling divine.

The caterpillars serve up sweet tea,
While ants dance a jig, full of glee.
Daisies laugh with their sunny faces,
Sprinkling pollen in joyous embraces.

A roach plays the drums, all six legs in sync,
The mushrooms cheer, giving a wink.
Everyone's swaying to nature's sweet beat,
In the heart of the realm, beneath tangled sheet.

At the end of the night, with stars above,
The critters all sigh, feeling the love.
In this green enclave, magic unfurls,
As laughter and joy fill the world in twirls!

Whispers from the Petal Path

Petals gossip in the gentle breeze,
Sharing secrets with curious ease.
"Have you seen the bee with a fancy new hat?"
"Why yes, and he buzzes like he's quite the cat!"

Butterflies flutter with tales to recount,
Of flowers that giggled, in a laughing mount.
"Last week, a snail tried to dance on a rose,
But tripped on his shell, oh, how that one goes!"

The daisies snicker at a clumsy bee,
As it tumbles and fumbles, wild and carefree.
"Just a bump in the air," giggles the grass,
"Tomorrow he'll charm, he just needs a pass!"

With each whisper, the colors collide,
In this petal path where joy confides.
Nature's own comedy, in every sprout,
Bringing laughter and warmth, no doubt!

Beneath the Oak's Watchful Eye

Under the oak, a meeting convenes,
Where wise old leaves count up the routines.
A raccoon grumbles for a midnight snack,
While a wise old owl gazes, keeping track.

Squirrels recount their daring throug,
In leaps and bounds, they give it a go.
"Did you see that jump? It was grand!"
"More like a flop," came the critters' band!

"Let's start a club," chirps a cheeky chive,
"Where every misstep makes us feel alive!"
The oak chuckles deep, roots twisting with mirth,
It's a comedy show right here on earth!

With acorns falling like laughter unchained,
Gathering joy from the frolics uncontained.
Beneath the oak, it's a party that flies,
Where whimsy runs wild, under vast, open skies!

The Journey of the Leaf

In a garden full of bling,
A leaf set off on its fling.
Chasing shadows, it twirled around,
Playing catch with the sun's rays found.

It jumped over puddles with glee,
Teasing ants, 'You can't catch me!'
But a gust of wind blew it away,
'Til it landed near a worm's buffet.

The worm just stared and gave a grin,
'You don't look very tasty, my win!'
The leaf just laughed, 'I'm not your meal,
I'm here for fun, not for a peel!'

So they rolled together on that ground,
A leaf and a worm, laughter profound.
In nature's dance, they found delight,
Who knew leaves could have such a night?

A Ballad of Nature's Hues

Once there was a flower bright,
Wearing petals, a wonderful sight.
It wore yellow, pink, and blue,
As it danced in morning dew.

A butterfly flitted by with flair,
'What a wardrobe!' it stopped to stare.
'But what's your secret?' it fluttered near,
The flower replied, 'No need to fear!'

'I mix colors in wild, silly dreams,
With a splash of laughter and vibrant beams.'
Said the butterfly, 'I'll join this spree,
Together we'll paint the world with glee!'

So they swirled in a joyful race,
Coloring clouds and the sun's embrace.
In nature's ballroom, they stole the show,
Reminding all that fun's a colorful glow!

Echoes Among the Ferns

In the forest where ferns softly sway,
A squirrel chattered, 'Let's play today!'
It invited a hedgehog, quite round and small,
To join in the fun, their laughter would call.

'What's the game?' the hedgehog did ask,
'Let's race through the leaves, it's quite the task!'
So off they zoomed, through twigs and grass,
Making a mess, oh what a blast!

As they tumbled and rolled, the ferns went wild,
Squirrel lost balance, and raccoon just smiled.
A chorus of laughter rose through the trees,
The forest joined in, swaying with ease.

Amidst all the giggles, they tripped and fell,
In the soft mossy bed, under Nature's spell.
Resting there, with smiles so wide,
Echoes of joy would forever abide.

Blossoms of Hope and Memory

In a garden where memories bloom,
A forget-me-not sang, chasing gloom.
It whispered tales of days gone by,
As daisies danced, reaching for the sky.

A lone bee buzzed, seeking some cheer,
'Tell me a story, lend me your ear!'
The flower then spoke of sunlit days,
Where laughter floated in curious ways.

Then came a breeze, tickling along,
'Your stories are sweet, they make me feel strong!'
The bee did a spin, with joy so grand,
Promising to share with all in the land.

So the blossoms united, in fun-filled chat,
Creating a symphony, how about that?
In nature's embrace, hope softly gleamed,
With laughter and memory, forever dreamed.

Tales from the Leafy Realm

In the forest where the squirrels play,
They argue about nuts throughout the day.
A wise old tree overhears their chat,
And chuckles softly, "What's up with that?"

The rabbits dance on meadow's green,
While birds gossip, oh, what a scene!
A dandelion joins with a twisty twirl,
As the sun shines bright, causing leaves to unfurl.

Mushrooms wear hats, trying to be grand,
While acorns joke, forming a band.
They strum on branches with musical flair,
Nature's own circus, like a wild fair!

So if you stroll through this leafy place,
Look closely, there's laughter in every space.
The trees might snicker, the bushes might smile,
Join the fun, stick around for a while!

Symphony of the Sunlit Canopy

Beams of sunlight, a spotlight on leaves,
Whispering secrets that nature weaves.
A caterpillar crawls up a branch,
Singing his tune, he takes a chance.

The flowers giggle, in colors bright,
Dancing together in pure delight.
But bees buzz loudly, making a fuss,
"Stop all the swaying! Get back on the bus!"

The wind joins in with a playful breeze,
Tickling the petals and rustling the trees.
A laugh out loud from the shy fern near,
"Join me, my friends, let's spread some cheer!"

With every rustle, with every sway,
Nature's a joker, come out to play.
The symphony plays, notes hug the sky,
In this sunlit canopy, we laugh and fly!

Echoes of Nature's Palette

In a garden where colors collide,
A flamboyant flower wears petals with pride.
With a wink and a twitch it starts to sway,
"Who needs a paintbrush when I'm on display?"

The thorns on the roses plan a scheme,
To trap all the bees that buzz and beam.
"Let's write a play, we'll steal the show,"
But the bees just laugh, "We've got pollen to tow!"

A gnarled tree giggles at the bee's silly dance,
"Nature's a jester, give laughter a chance!"
So they all join in, for a joke or two,
Colorful echoes in the garden's view.

With each blooming blossom, new tales unfold,
In this palette of nature, filled with gold.
So stop and listen, to what they say,
In this vibrant realm, join the fun today!

Chronicles of the Emerald Canvas

On the emerald canvas where critters roam,
Each brushstroke of green feels just like home.
A turtle poses like a statue quite still,
While the frogs croak a tune with a quirky thrill.

The butterflies twirl in a graceful arc,
Making the day glow like a sweet spark.
"Catch me if you can," they tease with glee,
As snails just smile, "No need to hurry!"

A playful raccoon with mischief aglow,
Plans an adventure with friends in tow.
They sneak through the bushes, giggling with glee,
In this canvas of joy, wild and free.

With every petal, and every rustle,
Life's funny moments turn into a bustle.
So wander through greens, let your heart dance,
In this emerald delight, take your chance!

Dancing Shadows Among the Leaves

In the garden where sunlight plays,
Frogs sport bow ties on sunny days.
A squirrel twirls in an acorn hat,
While daisies giggle, just imagine that!

Beneath the tree, a shadow glides,
A butterfly steals a ride with pride.
With each sneeze, a flower hops,
And laughter echoes when nature stops!

The wind whispers jokes to every sprout,
And grasshoppers dance without a doubt.
As petals get tickled by the breeze,
You'd think they're trained by circus bees!

So join the fun in this bright green scene,
Where vegetables wear coats, all fresh and clean.
In this leafy caper, there's room for cheer,
Come take a stroll, the fun is near!

Legend of the Canopy Creatures

In the branches where the monkeys swing,
A parrot recounts tales of silly things.
With every tale, the laughter grows,
As turtles juggle, stealing the show!

A raccoon sings while sipping a tea,
Dressed in a tux, looking fancy-free.
Meanwhile, snails race in slow-motion,
While worms groove, causing a commotion!

The owls hoot with wisdom so sweet,
Claiming moonlight makes the best treat.
While hedgehogs argue about who's best,
In this leafy kingdom, there's never rest!

But don't mistake this for just a dream,
For leaf-crazed creatures bust out the cream.
In the tale of the wise and the silly,
Come join the fun—it's worthwhile really!

The Lifestyles of Leaf and Petal

Under the sun, the leaves like to brag,
About their games and the fun they snag.
Petals wear shades, sipping nectar drinks,
Laughing at ants who ponder and think.

"Oh, look at me!" said the bold sunflower,
"Waving my arms for a bee to devour!"
While clovers giggle in a leafy lace,
Telling tales of a snail's funny race!

The rose took a selfie with a cool pose,
While daisies had dance-offs in neat rows.
In this garden life, it's all a delight,
Where the bees are DJs by day and night!

So hop on the vibe amidst the cheer,
Where flora sways without a single fear.
In the world of leaves, petals, and fun,
Every day shines bright under the sun!

Beneath the Canopy's Veil

Underneath where the shadows play,
The mushrooms gather for a feast each day.
A ladybug jokes with a sleepy slug,
While ferns flutter like a happy rug!

The tree frogs croak a comedic tune,
Drawn by the glow of a watching moon.
They dance on branches, oh what a sight,
While the crickets snap selfies at night!

With acorns rolling and laughter so sweet,
Every creature joins in this leafy treat.
As tendrils tickle the buzzing bees,
To celebrate life among the leaves and trees!

So come take a seat 'neath this green parade,
Where jokes blossom, and mischief is made.
In this realm of green, laughter's the key,
Beneath the canopy, wild and free!

Secrets in the Shade

In the garden where secrets hide,
Plants whisper tales with leafy pride.
A squirrel stole my sandwich, it's true,
He danced like a king, oh what a view!

The ferns giggle with every breeze,
While daisies gossip, if you please.
A mole made a tunnel that's quite a sight,
He claims he's the king of the night!

Beneath the sun, the veggies plot,
Tomatoes and peppers grow quite a lot.
In laughter of green, we find our fun,
Even cactus knows how to run!

So come on down, join the wild parade,
Where every petal is a charade.
In this green realm, we thrive and play,
With secrets galore, come swing by today!

The Lush Chronicles Unveiled

In a jungle where ivy twirls with glee,
A parrot laughed – is that a tree I see?
With every leaf, a story unfolds,
Of frogs in tuxedos and jaguars bold!

The plants host a party, it's quite absurd,
With ferns in hats, oh haven't you heard?
Peas in their pods roll on the ground,
Chasing sunbeams with merriment found!

A flower took a selfie—it's gone viral,
In a rosebud's outfit, it's quite the trial!
The bees are the bouncers, buzzing with flair,
While grasshoppers dance like they just don't care!

So take a stroll where giggles abloom,
Nature's hilarity sweeps through the room.
In this leafy laughter, we all belong,
Join the green chorus, let's sing along!

Greenheart's Legacy

In the heart of the forest, where giggles grow,
A wise old oak has much to show.
He tells of mushrooms with wild dreams,
And the antics of squirrels, or so it seems!

Beneath the fronds of a giant fern,
A snail in shades waits for his turn.
He claims he's the fastest in the race,
With a shell like a rocket, oh what a pace!

The daisies enroll in a ballet class,
While tulips cheer, "You've got some sass!"
Even the cacti play peek-a-boo,
With prickly arms and a grin, who knew?

In this green legacy, laughter's the key,
With roots tangled in fun, can't you see?
Join the dance of the leaves, embrace the jest,
In the legacy of green, we find our quest!

Roots of Life

Down in the dirt where the roots do mingle,
The garlic holds court, it's quite the jingle.
With potatoes cracking jokes all day,
Their humor's so underground, what can I say?

On a rainy day, the soil sings loud,
Worms throw a party, it's quite the crowd!
With raindrops falling like glittering gems,
The carrots grinning, "We are the stems!"

Those beans stretch up, trying to touch the sky,
While rhubarb's reciting a limerick high.
"Why did the tomato cross the road?"
To catch up with greens, it's quite the load!

So dig a little deeper, life's a show,
With roots entangled in fun's overflow.
In this underground world, joy is rife,
Come dance with the critters, it's roots of life!

Stories Untold

Beneath the canopy where shadows play,
Mushrooms tell stories in their own way.
"Why did we feast on a tasty shoe?"
Because it tasted great, that's what fungi do!

The dandelions laugh, they don't care a bit,
With wishes afloat, they think they're quite it.
In the breeze, they spin tales full of cheer,
Of love struck bees who forgot to steer!

The lilacs hum softly, weaving a tune,
Of nighttime adventures around the moon.
While the daisies prance with a wobble so sweet,
Chasing twinkling fireflies with tiny feet!

So gather 'round here, for laughter's pure gold,
In the stories of flowers, a world to behold.
With petals and roots, we share every plea,
These tales of the green will always be free!

Enchanted Fronds and Ferns

In a forest deep, the ferns do sway,
A dance of greens all through the day.
They gossip leaves in the summer breeze,
Telling tales of bugs and naughty bees.

The fronds wear hats made of dew and sun,
While blades of grass shout, "Hey, look, we're fun!"
With tiny giggles from mossy beds,
They plot mischief in their leafy heads.

The trees roll their eyes at the youthful spree,
"Oh, not again! Just let it be!"
But the ferns just laugh, twirling with glee,
In a world so green, wild, and free!

So come join the fun, take a look around,
Where laughter and greenery can always be found.
In fronds and ferns, life's a silly game,
In the mighty forest, we're all the same!

The Journey of Leaf and Light

A leaf stretched out towards the bright sky,
Chasing light beams while the clouds float by.
It tickles the sun with a glimmering jig,
While shadows grumble, "Oh, that's too big!"

With a wink at the breeze, it sways with cheer,
"Watch me shine! My time is near!"
The sun just chuckles, "What a show!"
As the leaf does its dance, putting on a glow.

Yet one day, it slipped with a comedic spin,
Landing on a toad who shrieked, "Not again!"
They rolled and they tumbled, such a sight!
By dusk, they were buddies—both filled with light.

So here's to the leaf and its journey anew,
To frolic with light, to dance 'neath the blue.
In laughter we grow, let the colors ignite,
For every small moment can spark pure delight!

Beneath the Canopy's Embrace

Underneath the trees, where shadows play,
The critters gather for a merry array.
A squirrel's on stage, performing a flip,
While birds chirp loudly, giving a quip.

The canopy sways, a roof of green hats,
Hiding the giggles of wise old bats.
As sunlight dances with laughter near,
And mushrooms whisper, "We've got nothing to fear!"

With squirrels playing cards and a raccoon sighing,
"Life is a game, and I'm just not trying!"
The trees are the judges, with leafy applause,
While the sun shouts, "Come on, let's take a pause!"

In this jolly place, they all join the fun,
Beneath the great trees, till the day is done.
So laugh with the leaves, let your spirit embrace,
For beneath the green canopy, there's infinite grace!

Vignettes of Verdure

In the verdant groves, where laughter roams,
The flowers converse in vibrant tones.
A daisy quips, "I'm smarter than weeds!"
While dandelions giggle, scattering seeds.

There's a witty cactus who wants to join,
But the flowers just laugh and say, "You'll purloin!"
"But I can be funny! A prickly delight!"
They answer, "Oh please, stay out of a fight!"

With cute little mushrooms, standing so stout,
They pop out and shout, "What's this fuss all about?"
The sun beams down, spreading joy in this lane,
As the vines intertwine, creating a chain.

So come to the grove where the green spirits sing,
In vignettes of life, let your heart take wing.
For here in the verdure, the laughter is clear,
Each moment a treasure, just waiting, my dear!

www.ingramcontent.com/pod-product-compliance
Lightning Source LLC
Chambersburg PA
CBHW071852160426
43209CB00003B/515